KUNG FU LULLABIES

KUNG FU LULLABIES

First published in England, 2004 by Ragged Raven Press
I Lodge Farm, Snitterfield, Warwickshire CV37 0LR
email: raggedravenpress@aol.com

website: www.raggedraven.co.uk

Kung Fu Lullabies
ISBN 0 9542397 7 6

Set in Arial.

Printed by Lithocraft, 35a Dane Road, Coventry, West Midlands
CV2 4JR

The Cantonese character on the cover means 'life force'.

Chris Kinsey

KUNG FU LULLABIES

Ragged Raven Press

For Ev & Liz

ACKNOWLEDGEMENTS:

Thanks to the editors of the following publications: *The County Times, Dream Catcher, Iota, New Welsh Review, Neon Highway, Orbis, Planet, The Penniless Press, Poetry Nottingham International* (especially for the Feature Poet selection, 2003), *Poetry Wales, Roundyhouse, Seam, Smiths Knoll, Smoke, Staple, Tears in the Fence, nthposition, and Wales & The Borders website;* and anthologies: *Dress of nettles* (Ragged Raven, 2004), *In the Criminal's Cabinet* (nthposition, 2004), *Reactions 3 and Reactions 4* (Pen & Inc Press, 2002 and 2003), *The Sensitively Thin Bill of the Shag* (The Biscuit Prize, 2003), *Adrift from Belize to Havana* (The Biscuit Prize, 2002), and *Beginnings* (The Housman Society, 2000); and to the organisers of performances: Academi, Charles Bennett & Ledbury Poetry Festival, Tim & Rina Clarke, Café Loco, Newtown, C.A.P. & Newtown Summer Festivals, David Caddy & Calder Bookshop, London, Brian Lister & The Biscuit Prize readings, North Shields & The Voice Box, London, Purple Patch/Poetry Monthly Convention, Wales region N.A.T.E. Conference and Great Oak Bookshop, Llanidloes

Peace Keepers won second prize in the 1998 Staple Open Competition judged by U.A. Fanthorpe and **Fighting with Steve** was a runner-up in the 1999 competition judged by Catherine Byron. **In the picture** was a runner-up in Ottakers Bookshop Competition, 2000, judged by Ruth Bidgood.

Special thanks to the **Arts Council of Wales** for the bursary which bought the time to write many of these poems.

Extra special thanks to: Evan Kinsey, Liz Hinkley, Gavin Pugh, Graham Mort, Todd Swift, Glenda Beagan, Jane Eagland, Gill McEvoy and Ty Newydd Writers' Centre, for feedback and support.

CONTENTS

Page

KUNG FU LULLABIES

A Kung Fu Lullaby

(For Lucy)

I've never faced a novice so young, so fierce -
a moment of cowardice
makes me want to hand you back.

Three weeks old;
fury fires your limbs,
charges your spine rigid.

Your perfect cries deafen midnight
till we tilt, heart on heart.
My hands let go

leave you balancing at low tide.

You shin along my ribbing
snuggle under my chin
subside into sobs and snuffles.

We bob in the shallows catching the swell
until we're afloat
billowing on big breaths.

I tell you in thoughts,
It takes time and lots of practice
to map a mind into a body.

2.00 a.m. Dad brings your feed -
you're stuck to my neck
like a snail on a hot wall.

Prised free,
we're both afraid
you're going to slip through our hands.

Osmosis

Sun streams under the door.
Sensing you're not asleep
I push the drifted silence,
see it's not tea you want.

You're cold but the bed is warm.
I reach a hand,
you let me cup your palm
stroke your stiff arms, kiss your cheek.

My tongue, trying to discover
who you are, licks grief
like a mother with a new calf.

Differences dissolve in
saltiness.
Only our sighs graze this
silence we secrete.

A Clearing

When my eldest son died last week

I ate –

started picking pieces of plasterboard
drilled my tongue into the cavity
wound fibreglass floss round and round.

I ground up breezeblock and brick –
licked every crumb –
chewed tables and chairs,
spat splinters.

In a cascade of foam,
I devoured the sofa –
all its flabby trampolinings,
sick bouts and Sunday snoozes.

I bit the taps off radiators,
gargled at their fountains.
Still thirsty,
I drained and buckled the tank.

Chipping the enamel off the bath gave me a jolt,

taste of iron returning to my blood,
prickled attraction and repulsion of mild steel
with the pins and plates bracing me, patching me
from times I was knocked down and smashed.

At 5.30, I quaffed the pilot light like a happy hour cocktail,
knew I must go deeper.

On my hands and knees I scratched aside tiles, slabs,
tasted oxides, alloys, amalgams –

I must excavate the gas main,
unleash the blue-hungry flames that snarl from the oven mouth.

Alwenna's flock
(Foot and Mouth crisis 2001)

The children charge the door and scatter.
Disinfectant in the air
catches up the second they stop.

Alwenna chooses playdough.
She pulls, kneads, squeezes,
then buries her hands.

The mixture's pinker than candy,
rawer than her mother's hands
after delivering lambs.

Rolling it flat,
she presses out a flock of sheep.
Nose to rump they follow the cutter's lead.

She peels them free;
muzzles shred, hooves fray.
She flings them into a pile

squidges harder, rolls smoother
cuts with tongue-biting care.
This flock struggles

to stand clear of the tackiness.
Generation after generation
stretches weakly and flops.

Smoke closes our valley.
I offer simpler shapes.
She slaps moon and star from my hand.

Two swans

shut their eyes against
shallow's melt.

Plying creaky feather shafts
nibbling filaments,

they rear and peel back
from perfect tattoos.

Rippling again they polish
their breasts, rub out their transfers.

Down curls off the surface
teasing trout to rise.

The current plucks loose quills
and scrawls urgent messages

in invisible ink.

An initiation into imaginary numbers
(For Michael)

Swiftly you sketch an axis,
make vectors take off

talk till dimensions blur
then tear the page.

I fold it into a dart
and consider possibilities:

air mapped by non-existent numbers,
flight paths plotted and tracked.

A skein of geese tows the dark
flies a ragged noose around our roofs.

Unflying it again, they find
their lines, their rank,

drive a wedge into the valley
forcing last daylight to spill

over the dam of hills
and gild the ox-bow lake.

Spoil tip

A wrong turn keeps us
climbing and twisting till
we're swept into the branches
of an old larch and all roads
are marked private.

I've stopped map-reading,
can't see for hurt.
A slipped remark set me drifting
through ten miles of chatter.
Realising we're lost

you reach across. The dog
interrupts, impatient to run
so we blink through rain,
clinker over slates riveted
with birch and pine.

I'm surprised to find them
splintered and thrown
into scallops of waste.
I feel shales squeeze again
heave into mountain.

Poised at the edge,
see-sawing on scree,
I'm closer than ever
to the long drop
into the valley's turned fields.

A Guide to Dragon Spotting

The secret is ...*shoulders.*

First, climb onto the shoulder
of Cader Idris and look down the mouth
of the Mawddach.

Be sure it's a low tide
when the sun is melting its treasure
and shadows with swag-bags creep over the land.

Dragons are very proud
of their slim, sinuous shoulders
and love to shimmy under the sands.

You might see them squirm in the slime
wearing the shot silks of sunset
siphoning spilled gold for their hoard.

They won't stay long,
they have to get back
to keep the Earth's core molten.

Lastly, take someone with you
because you'll only see
if you're squinting over their shoulder.

Desperado

Pushing through the hedge at three,
I hid amongst their hocks,
chuckled when tails whisked me.

Later, during my Cheyenne phase,
we stampeded on the plains.
Their vast eyes registered nothing
all their curiosity stranded to spittle
which cooled my naked back
left me slippery as a tickled trout.

Next summer the currency was dares.
I turned cowboy, took a big boy's challenge
to ride rodeo -
leaped from a broken-backed willow
to the shoulders of a red heifer.

Shock sealed us in a lumpy trot.

I don't remember the hurl -
just the immense heave of her outrage.

Just once

Dad took me out to the field.

We tunnelled through uncut hay
rolled dens with many rooms.
Cuckoo spit clung to the walls.

When we lay still and watched the sky
he said: *This is where we're coming to live.*

Years after we moved,
I searched for that meadow,

that sky.

So, you've never played hide & seek?

Hold out your arms.
Turn sideways. Surrender
when the fronds tickle your armpits.

It's damp in here
but we can lie back,
watch the sky through long lashes.

Bracken's good at keeping secrets.
So is hart's tongue.

Wait a little longer

slip into moss

sink under darkness.

Let's stay till we're anthracite.

Learning to read

When I was free of bed
in the afternoons, I dug.

With a red tin spade
I hacked and shovelled for Earth's core.

The clay sides of my craters crumbled
so I searched out treasure.

Mad for bits of blue, I sifted:

poison-glass sapphires
sky-coloured crocks

willow-pattern jigsaws
from the South China Seas.

Best was wiping mud from the dead
pirate's eye of a marble.

When I was seven, struggling to read,

pirates – Benjamin the Blue,
Gregory the Green and his griffin,

came to rescue me from Dick & Dora,
Janet & John, and Mummies & Daddies.

Sunday School

Sister Barbara let me keep my knife.
I was happy to let it sleep in its sheath.

Sister Mary wanted to confiscate it.
I teased its sharpness with my thumb.

One day I'd throw knives in the circus. I eyed up
the statues, their float away faces frightened me.

Father Patrick was going on about crucifixion
nerve by nerve, blood drop by blood drop.

Kevin passed out. I lent my blade to an older girl
who blinked into its light and painted her eyelids blue.

Wafers

All the way to the petrifying well I thrilled
at the thought of things turning to stone.

Tempted to risk a little finger to feel it
cool, calcify, grow brittle,

I chucked a stalk instead.
It floated. I waited.

Sinking it with a stick I got a splash –
we all stayed the same.

I wanted to fling my empty ice-cream cone
but was threatened with Africa's starving children,

so I scooped air, caught a few midges,
caught my aunt's attention.

Cross with her for sending me to the dark box
where I fluffed my lines and had to be prompted
to confess.

Cross with mum for capturing me,
fastening me into a butterfly white dress,
pinning the bodice chrysalis tight
over my wriggly chest,

I said: *I don't want this cornet*
it sticks to the roof of my mouth
like the host -

got a mouthful - *the sacred mystery,*
the body & blood of christ,
transubstantiation.

Mum, who never converted,
started up about how the baker she worked for
saved all the addled eggs for wafer mix.

She winked.
I hurled my cornet, a soggy shuttlecock
into brambles and wild garlic,

pictured it dissolving
faster than lost bones
wafering under the surface.

A small family history

I wanted to move out of monochrome,
pull mum and dad from the silhouettes
of mourners at the station.

Lifted aboard the magnesium-bright train
I tap-danced in my new Startrites
till mum snatched me onto a red seat.

It burned itchy like unshaven kisses.
I sat very still, fell asleep watching snakes
of cigar smoke swallow each other.

Cologne was a clattering of doors,
loudspeakers, luggage
and a hoik up steps to the cathedral.

The three of us stood on the platz:
shrunk by blackened spires that scratched the sky.
Mum's hands slipped my reins.

I left them standing in their honeymoon photo,
clopped off over the cobbles,
shuffled down the steps and found a smile.

The man lay in the rubble:
I was scared of cracks in the pavement,
but he laughed and we played clap-hands.

Then dad came and swung me high as a crane,
folded me into his coat and carried me
out of those cinders.

Oma's cellar
(Goch, Germany 1962)

Roots, sticks, willowherb –

lucky dipping through rubble
I reel out a yo-yo, polish
three dusty ball-bearings.

My German cousins begin the chase,
treasures tumble
back to the bomb site.

Busting out of a tackle,
I run over gardens,
lash some salvias with my stick.

Breathless, I drop down the cellar dug-out.

Detergent scums the stone sink
milky light laps its drain,
a slow tap beats.

The green mangle moves out of the shadows.
My arm, strong from the stick,
embraces the roller

elbow to handle we shuffle –

two steps,
            three steps,

I crouch into the dark.
The boiler rumbles steam.
Sunlight jemmies the door.

Should I give myself up or stay?

Oma's bloomers parachute above me –
I'm caught in the cat's cradle of her corsets.

AN INTRODUCTION TO COUNTY MAYO

1. Cottongrass, 1967.

Dad parked in a cloud.

I skipped a fence
braved the black bog
for three plumes
of waving cottongrass,
brushed the tufts up and down
my cheek, palm, arm.

Don't bring it near me, child!
Mrs Burke's smile vanished.
Fading like a headland in rain
she muttered,
Poor, poor starvation grass...

Her white head usually bobbed
telling me of homemade
soda bread, buttermilk, barmbrack,
hiding in the fuchsia hedge,
running wild down the mountain.

She wouldn't eat.

In her misty silence
famine came to our car picnic,
her anguish more barbed
than the fence wire which caught me.

I sat very still so no one would see
my jumper unravelling.

2. Camping on Achill Island, 1980.

County Mayo trips the whole Atlantic over its doorstep.

Air-hungry soils mop up cloud harvests
with acres of cottongrass.

Tourists, pilgrims and a few retired from exile,
keep shops and bars open.

Most sail away from this diluted land

except the fishermen
in their peat-black currachs
spilling starfish in the harbour.

TWO POEMS FOR TRUDY

A January walk

Arm-in-arm
we walk a line of low sun,
say in unison,
This is the tallest we'll ever be,
and start waving to our shadows.

Afternoon shift

Drifting with the dandelion seeds.
You chorus a stray, *This is the life.*
with, *It's a good life!*

And we buy the last courgette plant on the market,
try on perfumes,
detonate our cafetiere
as a mum dethrones a 'King of The Castle'
from the mall bench.

We watch a merganser and thirteen chicks
shoot the rapids past fumbling kayaks.

And still there's time to let a woodpecker's scarlet tail
direct us through falling petals
to watch horse chestnuts setting.

In the picture

All day we're buoyant through changing tides -

London arranging itself behind the shuffle,
the showers and April sun.

Our eyes keep losing focus on faces,
straying over roofs and domes

along the arms of cranes,
fishing skies for something of home.

Walking our course we talk and talk
until we stumble on a rainbow.

We're treading water in the flood.

Trouser bottoms carry smudges of chalk
and the olive branch is scuffed from the dove's beak.

The artist lies beside his creation and watches
feet traipsing pastels into neon eclipses.

Everyone's meeting someone and waving.

Slow-cruising car exhaust scatters crumbs.

Pigeons snatch light as they gobble,
their throats' tinctures releasing oils -

the sky, and its early stars,
still as an illumination in a *Book of Hours.*

Night drafts
(After M.C. Escher)

Creep down early
catch the kitchen floor still dreaming.

Shadows spill from cracks
scurry over checkerwork tiles.

What's left when the striplight stops blinking?

Sycamore seeds, a pen top
and a knotwork of newts

struggling for cover
before ink dries.

FOOTNOTE:
M. C. Escher (1898-1972)
Dutch graphic artist who became well known for prints that make use
of visual illusion.

Blue shift

Chagall's pictures suspend everything:

Horses, lovers, lilies, thieves.

The blues drain your tears;
you speak silently with his birds.

Light turns frisky under the fiddler's bow;
wing shadows spin the walls.

You're gone.

Windows open to the fairground screams
of swifts arriving.

FOOTNOTE:
Marc Chagall (1887 - 1985)
Russian-born painter and designer whose imagery draws heavily on
memories of Jewish life and folklore. His use of colour is extremely
powerful.

Missed

Distant telegraph wires
catapult thunder.

We stack our garden chairs
drive straight for the storm.

Through rapid blinks of wipers
we see ruts boil over.

Clear of the clouds
the ridgeway steams.

Strings of swallows shrug off drips
blotting themselves on sky.

What makes me sad is not
the signs of departure

but realising I haven't seen
swifts skim through this summer.

Ambush

Yellows and greens fly into finches.
Scarlet vibrates longest
then steadies into cotoneaster.

One dull Sunday
masked raiders held up our film.

Mum and I hid behind the curtains.
The waxwings had us surrounded.

She read aloud and I pictured
snow fugitives flying high
out of Scandinavian forests

blurring in North Sea spray
freckling the span of England
to invade our bush

as if some kind of lust for crimson
set a course far west of their territory.

Neighbours squeezed in behind our settee
stayed after dark dropping crumbs.

The birds stripped every berry then
flew forever out of the streetlamp's halo.

Bare twigs whisked at clouds,
whipped up snow too deep for school
and a flock of finches beat against mist.

Elegy for a bird

Forsythia's crestfallen
casting ragged yellow
for green.

Slate-smooth in my hands
I set you in a magnolia boat
amongst grey shales.

Celandines will spread hearts
over you and yield to yarrow
then spark again next Spring.

A stand of tulips carouse the dew
a few share your orange blush.
Wild cherries – prunus avium –

send petals, singly
like the spots of pearling
on your nape.

Soon they'll blizzard, drift
into the lines of your wing coverts
and fly.

Two Welsh poppies cock their heads
so does your hen.
She calls and calls.

Your missing syllable
shuffles the rhythm of the roll-call
making us muddle all names.

Celebrating Solstice at Kilpeck Castle

A sudden turn onto the stubble field
unleashes dogs to pheasant scent.
They spiral over the snow
to a hollow where slush gathers
and tracks vanish behind the bared
teeth of blackthorn.

Our slow, slithered prints make
marls bleed under the ice-scars.
Pausing at the moat, a toecap
nudges apart frozen continents.
Our faces ripple on the surface.
One by one we jump the straits.

On the rampart, huddled against
the crumbling tower, we light tilted candles.
Our palms play roaring flame as
a kestrel, soaring from churchyard yews,
lifts the horizon -

wet mistletoe winks at the sun.

Out with the greyhound

Inland
light and form were fixed in reflections
now we're in a white-out of drizzle
and things turning: tide, day, year,

the hound's paws spin pebbles,
curl along the waves as she raises plover.

The rivermouth is awash with swallowed sky.
In the chew of cross-currents
oysters pan for colour, dull pearl
answers the white lead of the horizon.

With a gleam of pink
the sun dissolves cloud.

We run up a sand dune
the hound sees the dart of a plane.

Racing its vapour trail along the foreshore
she thunders over ribbed flanks –

where the huge sandhound is sleeping.

I keep meaning to

I never quite trust my wolf
not to eat my pretty things
so, whenever I go out,
I shut him from the hearth.

He always gets into my bed.
I find him, head on the pillows,
paws crooked over the coverlet,
often as not, wearing a silly grin.

Shouldn't have encouraged him really.

I keep meaning to tell my granddaughter.

Oyster

How long did you sit in the shallows
taking the Atlantic's pulse?

Was it just for fun
you siphoned shimmer from the skies?

Did your secret break out in bubbles?
Blow on butterflies' wings?

Did you burst against a starling?
Get swallowed by a pigeon?

Do you splash or drown in oil spills?
Are you buried with the opals?

Solo on St. Valentine's Day

Half-day shopping -
closed signs swing askew.

Man and amaryllis
stand either side glass.

He sends smoke ciphers,
the red flower blows kisses.

High-stepping down the street
he conducts a concrete-mixer
through the last waltz.

Sleet taps his shoulder -
he starts a new dance.

...something blue

It's the wedding season again,
talk of outfits, etiquette, *expense.*

It'll be my go in a minute.
The turn comes like a tackle.

Do you regret getting wed?

No, only the blue eye-shadow.

Didn't it go with your outfit?

It went pretty well
with my new jeans.

The women in work
had a whip-round

then got cross about
things not being 'proper'.

They barged the door.
Yvonne buckled my knees

Denise knelt on my arms
I lay still and shut my eyes.

After that, it was a laugh.

Night out

The kebab van's just
a smell in the gutter.
Distant high heels
are striking half past two.

The man in the shop doorway
zips up, rubs his hands and says,
*I could just fuckin' strangle
some bastard now.*

My grin see-saws between
Oh yeah? and *Don't pick me.*

And he doesn't.

The consolation of handbrake turns

The convoy parks nose-to-nose.

It's a stand-off -

stereos synchronize,
body kits rock & roll.

Mirrored windows
pick up the girls first.

Clicking fingers,
four of them strut into the corral of cars

and dance

perfectly in step

perfectly in time

the way they practised
in breaks at the curtain factory.

The cyclops' eyes under their crop-tops
wink and pull a crowd.

The lads honk for more
but stiletto rain drives them off.

Later,

just the rhythm of the revs

the squeal of summer skids

fish-tailing on the banks of the Severn
    red-lining
        white-lining

until the night is hoarse.

Afterwards

In the vacuum made by sirens, the bus waits
on a policeman's wave.

Perhaps all a driver did was sneeze
and wheels took a course of their own.

Crash barriers buckle from curving white lines
to fields smoking with pollen.

Beyond, the river stretches and yawns up
a summer island of purple foxgloves.

Shifting through diesel fumes
the tanker scrubs the carriageway.

We splash through a misty halo,
arrive where lime trees

swing thousands of censers
shock-pale rugosas saturate the air

rain can't hold back any longer.

Late shopping

Ten shuffles along
your shoulders look familiar
but wrongly set. It's your voice though

requesting, *Cheapest whisky.*
Clinking the change you turn to give me
a prodigal smile.

Leading me down the aisle
you start unbuttoning your shirt,
That night four years ago -
I didn't stand you up...

A scar skids past your navel, rears up
to spit your right nipple at my eye.

The highway's imprint lasts
in the tread of old sutures.

You press me to touch
but I pull back.

Composing yourself as a dancer again,
I watch you arrange your limp.

Your exit blurs on the grainy screen,
cuts as the door closes.

Fighting with Steve

We're standing face to face
holding hands edge to edge
like blades.

Carving a circle between us
we smile, glide into easy orbit.

Teasing to distraction
our eyes glint as we upset
each other's tides.

If I fall into your gravity
you lock my wrist
and the bolts are thrown on every joint.

All I've left is my bite -
grinning,
I mime gnashing, nibbling.

When pain surges I beg *mercy.*

Starting again, on the other foot,
I catch you.

You plead, not for release,
but *harder, harder, harder*
until your carpals are rattling.

What if the insulation
of flesh is gone,
and I'm down to the mesh
of nerves on bone?

I have to hold on,
can't bear to drop the digits
like a puzzle shaken from its box.

Escape

We're used to faces at the window,
comments from off stage -

the kung fu carries on
but last night

we all stopped striking,
gathered round the moon

watched it ward off the hill
and spin clear of clouds.

Trapped in double panes at lights out,
it multiplied into a chain of moons

and scaled free.

Wind chill factor

A couple coming out of Kwiksave
take their carriers to a flatbed Ford.

The fat woman's wearing a summer dress.
It's December and the shadows
try not to look up it.

Her hem's set like the floor of a carousel.
Everything hangs awkwardly.
Gravity's not her friend.

They stow groceries on the seat.
A terrier leaps off the dashboard
loops the loop, muffing her hands.

The man brings a crate
plays handrest steadying her climb,
the dog jumps on the shopping.

The woman sits, legs splayed on the loadbed,
arms outstretched whilst he lashes her
tenderly to the cab.

When the engine starts
I look at the darkening clouds ahead,
wonder how far they're going.

She's already swede-cold.
I shout, *Give her a blanket*
into exhaust fumes.

Eczema

Tyres slap in the sweat of melting tar.
She cycles into the shade behind houses,
wild barley ratchets her spokes.

Two boys swing out of hazels,
the bigger speaks so softly she stops.
Why you wearing gloves?

She's forgotten. He points.

Peeling back a white glove
his tender palmistry traces
her crazed life-line back to the pulse.

Afternoon fractures into blue light.
The boys drop her hand
to chase passing sirens.

Gloving the tingle,
she squeezes hot grips
and rides the trailing silence.

A smell of petrol

A stranger, you come in late, glazed with rain.
Others welcome you,
dry you off with stories

of grandmothers baking bread
children picking poppies in cornfields
sisters who live on opposite ends of a rainbow.

When the stories finish
we place paper on your knee.

Your smile dies. Very meekly you say,
I can't write.

We go into a rigmarole of reassurance.

Hunching round a pen,
you carve between the lines.

Refining memory turns you to a still,
your pores pump sweat.

I can't forget the smell of petrol.

When I was a soldier ....
I saw petrol turn a boy into a bomb.

Sighing, you suck it all back into your chest.
Your last sob stoppers it.

There was nothing I could do.

Out on the street the rain has stopped.
Every drain exhales the smell of petrol,
every puddle is rainbow-filmed.

At the heart of the memorial garden
damp asphalt smells stronger than roses.

Progress

At our first class you stopped us in the hall
demanding, *Baccy.*

Then you'd stand in the doorway asking,
Anybody want to buy a pair of size 9 shoes?

October rain drove you to tap the door before tea
and whisper, *Will you let my mate out soon?*

At Solstice you came in to a welcome -

wrote about *hands dancing to music*
led us down *the road which looks round bends.*

Told us of *Working dawn to dark,
making the M6 for McAlpine.*

New Year saw you in trouble with your hostel.

Stamping and shouting like Rumpelstiltskin
you threw your pen, but showed us

the mountain with its parachute in Hiroshige's print
described Klimt's shed as *washed in the colour of leaves.*

When we jinxed a box with curses
you lifted its lid with broken fingers

stroked its lacquered inside and said:
I could live in here curled up like a mole.

Late

You stride in late by weeks.

One by one our faces
look back from your passing navel-stud.

You take your place.
Tattooed flames flicker blue-black, blue-black
under the fingers strobing your abdomen.

I finish the lesson.

We wait as coke goes flat,
crisp bags stop their crackle
and the last person closes the door.

Swear you won't tell!

Smiling, you pull your scan from a back pocket.
A peep through a keyhole.

You make my finger trace
skull, spine, placenta.

But my eye only reads scuffs and comet-tails.

Something's wrong

The crowd streams past,
we both break into broad smiles

but something's wrong.

Too much deliberation in your stance,
too much tilt -

I remember your face
but your name's gone -

I say it
and memory filters back.

You used to teach me didn't you?

I nod, ask, *What's happened?*

Brain haemorrhage,
comes out loud and clear,
but *Last Sep...*
                    tem...
spaghettis into silence.

And you wait a few breaths
for your old voice to return.

I went altogether twice.
Up there didn't want me -

Down there didn't want me neither -
So I've come back.

I think of all your connections lost,
hard-won words spilled.

I want to learn again.
Then you falter.

We start, not with Macbeth,
but by making a map.

Last count

Under the weight of watching
the clock hands jerk the last quarter.
Visiting conversation dries.
More X-ray than man, your ghost sigh
steals all stares. My eyes ride the angle

of your pillows, rest at your identity.
The name recalls your face full-fleshed,
flushed, restores the volume on years
of chanting tables, formulae, rules -
you bellowing, *Show your workings,*

until your spit sizzled on the backs of my hands,
floated the ink off numbers I copied.
Now your mouth's set to zero
and so dry we can't hear you whisper.
Your workings are all on show.

Graphs waver a course between
the parallel lines of your bed.
Clipboards monitor your progress.
Someone's counting the cost of your care
dreaming of minuses making a plus.

INDUSTRIAL RELATIONS

1. Morning Break

Scrape and flick of fast ladles
clatter of crockery on stainless steel
cook bangs a handle, and shouts:

Eh up, flasher's back in t' snicket!

She fish-slices the air.
Everyone pours to the windows –
'Confec' are clearly back from months in Coventry -
all lines unite jeering and gesturing.

A slow-eater, I hold the table
against the canteen capsizing,
carry on with my scrambled egg
and fingering bits of fag packet.

Night shift's game scores curl in the ashtray
Pencilled names unfurl:
Flash, Chop, Mugger…

I wonder what happened to Iron Bar Billy?

Haven't seen him since the strike –

we'd get off picketing
to play Scalextric Grand Prix
in a back bedroom in Kettlethorpe.

2. Rehabilitation

Pumping jelly into pork pies
you were always singing
songs from before you went down:

How do you do what you do to me,
I wish I knew -

When we crossed to your line
and watched you inject a pie crust
we wondered.

One time Lisa came straight out with it:
That bloke wot you axed,
wor his brains like that?

You just turned up your smile
and sang; *If I knew*
how you do it to me
I'd do it to you.

Stove-gazer

The coals sighed and rumbled - I stared at their shadow-play
till my tongue teased towards the mica window,
craving the taste of fire.
I leaped into the roar,
skipped flame-licks,
caught the rush and rose in blazing updraught.
Taller, lighter,
I turned chimney spark,
re-ignited soot somersaulting out to frost light.
Speck, spiralling on the night,
summoned by white birch
beyond furnace-glow or lanterns,
back before sticks branded campfires
– further –
before trees were oak, pine or scrub willow.
I drifted into horsetails, cooled in ferns,
fell into the press of a long sleep.
Sometimes, now,
I wake into a body on fire,
sinews crackling, solar plexus sparking,
skin flaking like schist or a salt-lick of sand.
My toes blister and weep resin.

Daddy's been a-hunting

Last time I saw you asleep in a moses basket,
a gust of wind crowned you with lace knickers.
Your mum snatched them from your frown:
If it weren't for these
you mightn't be here.
She laughed, lassoing the clothes horse.

There were rows.
She left, taking all her lace.

Now it's just the two of you.

Chicken ribs are set aside like impossible airfix,
dad rolls a scotch egg from its plastic bag,
and hopes you've had enough.
Slicing with his Swiss Army Knife
he makes the mistake
of enthusiasm

Pork or egg?
Egg or pork?

More! You squeal, *More!*

Sausage meat spraying from your chuckle
sticks to your rabbit-patterned jumper.

The night before full moon

The moon is up early
blinking through lashes of fir

it spotlights our walk
then jumps onto the branches of a sycamore

climbing clear of the horizon
it snoops on the sun and blushes.

Planes over charcoal hills
pull last threads of sunset
through the blueing west.

Clay

Forget Adam.

Forget: spare ribs, snakes, knowledge -

the fall.

Tumble with me.

Start over again.
I'm clay.

Mould my outlines
with your inquisitive touch.

Let your rhythm find my pulse.

When I'm complete, but still spinning,
let your hands slip back.

Glaze me with your smile.

Scribe

All morning
a money spider's been writing
the outer reaches of thoughts in my hair.

Now it abseils to the page
and runs away.

First day of summer

The river's having a lie-in.

Mist swells.

Two boys thread their feet through alder roots,
grip tight, once the net's swallowed
it's too heavy for one.

They sway into contest,
their breaths thicken to whispers -
Massive, this one's massive!

The wash is all from the fish.
Rising again and again,
it snaps its swirl.

Gaping mouths clear the mist.

By late afternoon the fish is back, basking,
head of the posse who stick in the river's current
like a wishbone.

Windflowers

Sitting among wild anemones,
sky so blue it makes her stare,

a flake of ash slips

through tiny horse chestnut leaves.

She thinks of letters torn and burnt.

Across the park,
another girl clings to the back of his scooter,
laughing as they brush down cherry blossoms.

Weather vanes

Yesterday's fog extinguished colour,
the only birds were puffed blackbirds

and woodcock returning to roost
like flung sods of peat.

Today's sun ignites
last year's bracken.

Two red kites spiral then hover
buckling under the span of blue.

Though our feet crunch ice nails
gorse flames with new blooms.

Painting the Dyfi Estuary

The river unscrolls
to a tug of white sky.

Loaded reeds lay curlew colours
over land and estuary.

Behind the calligrapher's hand
migrations switch,

wintering geese hunker
behind shelduck and oystercatchers.

In the last cove before the harbour
sleet sharpens strokes –

a vagrant egret flies
the brimming ink-stone.

In the park

Free from exams,
a couple are learning love.

Legs entwined in lotuses,
they rise from their own star

to a single-point kiss
then shift, divide.

He tilts the bottle for her,
she for him,

sipping, they read from
'First Love, Last Rites'.

Later they'll light a fire
to bring down the starlight.

August

Young men snap saplings,
whip flaps of bark,
stropping up nerve.

Heat makes all things volatile
cracks distant thunder.

They fence,
parry,
scourge sweat,

light the sticks
stoke fires with catalogues
and vodka.

In the morning, bins smoulder,
strewn bottles distil dew.
A breeze riffles charred pages.

Rain

Spendthrift cloud –
last night's ravers
race to huddle under the bridge.

Spouting rain spatters clothes,
fibres shrink;
muscles tighten.

Two zig-zag the silver park
till one wields his skateboard
like a shield.

The other catches him,
hugs him,
stumbles him against a beech trunk.

They kiss a kiss
that should stop the storm.
Come with me now –

If they say anything,
I'll flatten them.
Javelin-thin, he runs slant to the rain.

The other stays,
clutching his board like a raft.
He pulls his black hood lower.

Air's astringent as aftershave
with nettles and flowering lime.
Gutter-gossip roars in downpipes.

Taxi

We clean the fleet on Sundays.

Got a powerhose for the outsides,
but the insides....

Saturday nights people phone
when they've had a skinful.

They want to eat chips and curries
and shag in the cab.

Some of them say,
D'you mind pulling over?

I look 'em in the eye in the mirror
and say, *Not if you don't mind me watchin'.*

There's girls, regular,
saying they're skint,
offering to pay in kind.

Me, I need the fare.

Waiting in a one shelter town

I squeeze onto slats that don't look spat on
or blistered with bubble gum.

A three year old's being cross-questioned:
What colour's that crane?
Not looking he says, *Yellow!*
then cracks under pressure - *Red!*

What do you think we'll see on our journey?
Silence…
Cowboys! ricochets off the walls.

Thumb cocked over littlest fingers he shoots
his mum with both barrels,
runs into the road and won't give himself up.

My eyes ride the range of spilt takeaways,
call and response graffiti:
tags, slags, praises, threats -
Edward Hamer must die!

The big concerns:
Why War?
Why do fat bitches wear Spandex?
Because we want to.

I wish my missus was as dirty as this shelter,
smudges into roof soot,
jumps onto the bus with me
and paces my journey like a 'Wanted' poster.

The three year old presses his face to the window
squinting for cowboys in the long grass of the plain.

Angels

The bruise-blue stripes of bare mattress
remind her of her gran's bed.

His fingers unpick dope from clingfilm
as Hendrix jangles through speakers.

Her eyes climb the walls,
search for a way out.

Boots thud down attic stairs.
The door splinters open.

Angels swoop wielding bike chains
and kitchen knives.

She runs into the night.

Catching her breath on the last bus
she reads *Hells Angles* on a wall

and laughs loud enough for the couple
in the back seat to stop groping and stare.

Late blackbird singing

A handful of April hail
grazes glass.
We break from our meal,
see the window is
a welder's mask.

Outside a deeper carbon
soots the dark.
A blackbird strikes
a song so clear
walls vanish.

Our cockatiels fling themselves
on the rayburn's sleepy thermals,
swoop incandescent loops
under the strip light,
land, shrieking, on the sash bar.

Hissing, they join molten cheeks,
dip flaming crests, vent out tails.

Silence folds back with closing wings.

The intruder is doused by the rain.

No need now to blow on our soup.
The cock struts his boundary
the hen flies to our table.
They play kiss chase through breadcrumbs.

Bathers

Goose pimpled boys queue on the bank.

Launching themselves on lungfuls

they fly

curl to foetus

plunge breech.

Every loud slap claps out cheers
swallowed in the wash.

The river runs rings round each one.

Cold cure

Wringing a lemon to pith
I rinse the sting from my fingers.

Movement flits my eyes to the eaves –
a goldcrest works gutter moss

her pale yellow crown
strikes the early moonlight

till I cry out with scalding.

Peace keepers

Once again the flat is cold as ash
mother's nose is pinched and pink,
her shivering hands are blue.

Our breath fumes like smokers'
as she rolls me into the blanket.
But soldiers, stamping on street corners,
are the only ones with cigarettes.

She speaks in fingers and whispers.
The blanket is warm,
but it prickles.

She carries me down,
leaves me under the stairs,
goes to join food queues.

I wait, sometimes till dim light darkens,
watching the spider on her ropes.
When footsteps shake walls
she knots tight to a corner.

I mustn't cry out
otherwise more windows will break,
more ceilings fall
and soldiers, sick of screams,
will come clubbing through the rubble,
keeping the peace.

Children of parents on crutches

set off early,
walk fast,
tease stones and cans,

pound walls,
shoot the moon
through basketball mouths.

Children of parents on crutches
meet up late.

Don't speak about it,

but score tarmac,
skate under streetlights,
deep-breathe frost....

These are our charms.

Why are you so long in the bath?

Sometimes, drowsing in a hot bath,
my feet remember being young and swim
like salmon back to the source.

The river's cold clamps my legs,
but soles dive, sure as the shoals
that dart the clear current.

Downstream toes unplait, paddle silt,
emerge clay-coated and cloudy,
enjoy the tickle of minnows sucking them clean.

A disturbance of larvae thickens the water,
feet are alert for
lashing leech and lamprey -
they remember crushing the bullhead.

Sick with shock, they're suddenly sensitive
to sharp grit, the shrimp's rodeo.
They stumble back begging for pardon,

plunge under lacewing foam,
need no coaxing to be soaped and anointed
and slipped into sheets.

Svalbard

80 degrees North.
Midnight sun makes June unblinking.

First trip out we ride the thaw-tide's swell
towards The Snow Queen's iceworks.
Source of all crystal.
Every blue.

In tundra bays we step around
the scruffy fluff of nesting eider,
over logs from Siberia's rivers
sheltering resting walruses.

We climb to the great skua's plateau,
keeping the heart alert for the groan
of a glacier calving, for the polar bear's
ambush down sculpted slipways.

Reindeer stamp on ice-mirrors
shatter reflections into lichen and moss.
Seals watch the zodiac nosing through ice-floes.

Leaving, we take no trophies.

Bones of whalers splinter through permafrost.
Beside the blubber ovens a skull
stares from its look-out.

Blacksmith

The shed is shadowy with carbon fur.
A girder screams through saw's teeth.

No one hears me come in.

I squint to make silhouettes into men.
Dad's master of the indigo flame.

He joins edges of melted steel with
the firework that sparks forever.

If you stare you go blind.

Swarf scuffs under my sandal.
I sniff hot iron, wait for his mask to drop,

claim my thruppence,
run back to the street.

Pulp

Sniffing another wayside shrine,
the dog reads from mildewed messages
and freesias suffocating in plastic.

On the other side of the track
centre-spread girls, snagged on brambles,
keep on smiling.

Sprayed with shot, and slung
over the gate, a sex-doll
blows us vinyl kisses.

We walk away from the wheelspin drag
down to where horsetails flourish along the stream
and the dog emerges shaking off rainbows.

Ragged Raven's poetry publications:

Seven League Stilettos by Jane Kinninmont £7   ISBN 0 9542397 6 8
The whole feel of the book had a spark of something that was special...pictures that could not be caught with a camera. Reach

Vanishing Point by Tony Petch   £6.50   ISBN 0 9542397 3 3
...throughout the book there are flashes of genius as insight combines with surprising expression. **www.suite101.com, Cold Mountain Review**

People from bones by Bron Bateman and Kelly Pilgrim
£6.50 ISBN 0 9542397 0 9
The book is the work of two poets who tackle life with wit and sympathy ...Together they have created an excellent collection and deserve a wide audience. **New Hope International**

the cook's wedding by John Robinson   £6.99   ISBN 0 9520807 8 8
A poet with immense talent, a poet at war with himself. **Voice & Verse**
Accessible, visual and rich. **The New Writer**

Saturday Night Desperate (anthology 2003)   £6   ISBN 0 9542397 2 5
A whole host of good things...emphasising the excellence of contemporary poetry today...You'll read it again and again. **bluechrome**

The promise of rest (anthology 2002)   £6   ISBN 0 9520807 9 6
This is one of those anthologies where you don't look for what's good, but what is exceptional ... an excellent collection. **Purple Patch**

Red Hot Fiesta (anthology 2001)   £6   ISBN 0 9520807 7 X
Strong, tight and characterful. **New Hope International**

Smile the weird joy (anthology 2000)   £6   ISBN 0 9529897 6 1
An overflowing cornucopia of all that is best in contemporary poetry... there is delight on every page. **Poetry Monthly**

Old songs getting younger (anthology 1999)   £6 ISBN 09520807 5 3

Ragged Raven Press also produces quarterly poetry magazine, *iota.*